G00242300

= LETTS =
Contemporary Crafts

Painting Furniture

JACLYNN FISCHMAN

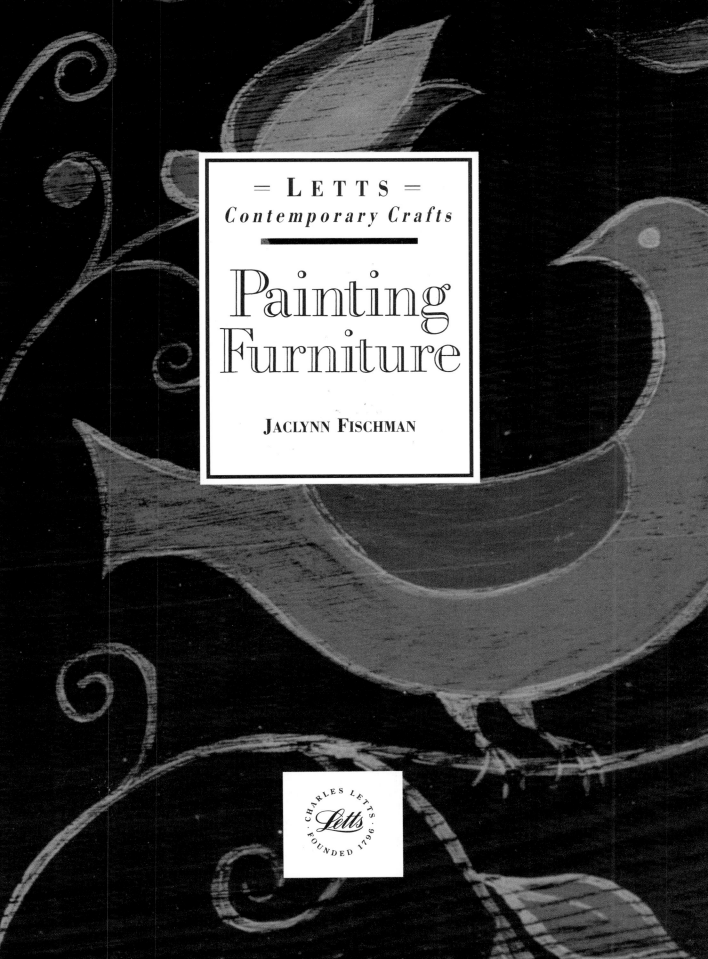

= **LETTS** =
Contemporary Crafts

Painting Furniture

JACLYNN FISCHMAN

CHARLES LETTS
Letts
· FOUNDED 1796 ·

First published 1992
by Charles Letts & Co Ltd
Letts of London House, Parkgate Road,
London SW11 4NQ

Designed and edited by
Anness Publishing Limited
4a The Old Forge
7 Caledonian Road
London N1 9DX

ISBN 1-85238-168-X

A CIP catalogue record for this book is
available from the British Library.

'Letts' is a registered trademark of
Charles Letts & Co Ltd

Editorial Director: Joanna Lorenz
Project Editor: Polly Boyd
Text Editor: Judith Casey
Creative Director: Peter Bridgewater
Photographer: Sue Atkinson

Printed and bound in Spain by
Printer, industria gráfica s.a.

AUTHOR'S ACKNOWLEDGEMENTS

*I would like to thank Sarah Greaves Stewart for introducing
me to this project; Elle Frieda of World of Interiors
magazine for her time and research support; Florence de
Dampenir, who I have never met, but whose beautiful and
informative book on the history of painted furniture was an
excellent reference source; Stanley and Joanne Fischman,
whose unconditional support never ceases to amaze me; and,
finally, Simon and Deborah Vermooten for their guest room,
their computer, and most of all their patience.*

Photographs on page 9 supplied by Ingrid Mason Pictures.

CONTENTS

INTRODUCTION

HOW MANY TIMES have you stacked magazines on top of an old wooden coffee table to cover the ever-growing number of scratches and stains; moved that lone wooden chair to a different place in the room, wondering why you haven't just thrown it out; or buried the chest of drawers that you inherited from an ageing relative under another storage box in the garage? Every home has at least one or two pieces of wooden furniture that have become old and tired. They get moved from room to room, eventually making their way into a garage, basement or attic where they get buried under countless other forgotten items of varying sentimental value. What this book aims to do is to motivate you to take a new look at your old relics or to seek out new pieces from an unfinished pine warehouse or second-hand furniture shop, and hopefully, by offering you a basis of useful techniques and helpful hints, inspire you to give new life and personality to those old faithfuls.

The idea of painting furniture is by no means a new concept in decorative finishing. For thousands of years it has been a well-documented and appreciated art form which can be traced back as far as the Ancient Egyptians. Their technique of coating wood with a sealant similar to a 'gesso', and then applying pigmented stains to the surface as it dried, is seen on many of the chairs, coffins

. . . .

This finely painted cupboard is boldly decorated with fruit and flowers in the traditional European style of the nineteenth century. (Photograph by kind permission of McWhirter Antique Furniture.)

and burial objects found by archaeologists. The technique has evolved and, although synthetic materials are now used, it is still practised today.

Oriental lacquer work, which is credited to the Han Dynasty (206 BC – AD 25), has enjoyed a similar evolution, and is considered to be the foundation of contemporary furniture painting. The Chinese decorated wooden furniture and objects with layer upon layer of a liquid composition called lacquer, which was based primarily on the sap of sumac plants and coloured red with cinnabar or black with charred bone meal. As many as ten to twenty layers of lacquer coating were applied, with a drying time of more than twelve hours between each coat, after which the detailed decoration was added. Lacquered furniture and objects can be traced to every successive dynasty from that time, and were eventually introduced to Europe in the late 1600s when Louis XIV received a gift of two small pieces of furniture from the Queen of Siam. It soon became *de rigueur* for royalty and nobles to have at least one room with an oriental décor, fitted completely with lacquer. The Dutch East India Company could not import pieces quickly enough to meet the demand, and due to the nature of the art, as production time was slow and laborious, shipping schedules were often delayed indefinitely. European cabinet-makers, in order to help to satisfy the impatient market, tried importing lacquered and decorated panels and attaching them to a prefabricated framework, but the panels did not adapt well to the European furniture designs, and there were often visible seams and inconsistencies in colours and patterns.

The obvious solution was to simulate the lacquering technique within Europe. The first success in domestic manufacturing was in France. The technique, called

This games cabinet-on-stand from the early nineteenth century is a fine example of Chinese lacquer ware. (Sotheby's.)

. . . .

A fine Edwardian painted commode (1903) illustrates the British furniture painter's fondness for the styles of the eighteenth century. (Sotheby's.)

'*vernis Martin*' after the three Martin brothers who invented it, began a trend that swept Europe. Artisans of every country began to adapt their own styles and techniques to those of the French. Detailed decoration and masterful painting began to adorn the furniture, walls and floors of the palaces and stately homes of the European royalty and nobility.

Decorative furniture painting travelled as far as Russia, brought back by Peter the Great who became enamoured with oriental-style objects collected during his travels through Europe. But it was the mountainous regions of Scandinavia and Switzerland, cut off from the influences of central Europe by the long cold winters, where the art developed to one more accessible to the masses. With these groups came the evolution of folk style art, now a recognized decorative style with its bold and unpretentious shapes and colours.

Pattern books are often good source material for designs, such as these folk designs from Scandinavia.

The styles may have varied, but the development of the art of painting furniture has been enriched by almost every country and culture at some time in its history. The work of today's artists is generally very vibrant and expressive, and often has a whimsical or satirical twist, and although the art is constantly moving in new and different directions, it is practised to the same exceptional level of finish as it was at the height of its popularity in the eighteenth century. The variety of work in the Gallery section on pages 18–27 illustrates how unlimited the sources of inspiration are and how unrestricted this craft is as a means of expression. But don't feel daunted by the creations of these artists and designers. When you look at the Project section of the book, you will begin to see that by following the step-by-step instructions and the techniques outlined, it is possible to achieve professional results very simply. Inspiration can be found in the most obvious sources: fabric, carpets, patterns on plates or silverware, and even things around you such as fruit, flowers and leaves have the potential to be decorative elements in a design. If you are still feeling uninspired, your local library will most likely have pattern books from which you can adapt designs.

So look around and find that piece of furniture that is crying out for a fresh identity or a splash of colour or style, or take a trip to a used-furniture or unfinished pine shop and add something new and special to your home. You will find that there is a definite feeling of satisfaction from having created something lasting that is guaranteed to provoke surprised admiration from family and friends. Then, when you are asked, 'What a great piece of furniture, where did you get it?', you can honestly answer, 'Oh that? It's been around for ages.'

MATERIALS AND
EQUIPMENT

THE MATERIALS and equipment required for painting furniture are relatively inexpensive and readily available in art and craft shops and hardware or do-it-yourself stores. This section covers all the various types of paint and varnish available, and the basic painting equipment that you will need.

PAINT

There are two basic types of paint, water-based (emulsion, vinyl enamel or latex), and oil-based. Both varieties come in a flat/matt, satin or gloss finish. For painting furniture, a flat or matt finish paint is most preferable, as decorative work will adhere better to a duller basecoat. A gloss shine can always be applied after the decoration using a poly-gloss varnish.

Most projects in this book specify water-based acrylics and emulsions. Although oil-based paints tend to render a more brilliant colour with a stronger finish, water-based paints are easier to work with, as they can be thinned with water, and require only warm, soapy water for cleaning up and washing brushes. Oil-based paints require a solvent, such as white spirit, for thinning and cleaning, and whereas an oil-based paint will take anywhere from 8 to 12 hours to dry, a water-based coat will generally dry in less than 2 to 3 hours.

With all paints, allow each coat to dry thoroughly before applying successive coats, as the damp layer may wrinkle or bubble under the new layer if it is not allowed full drying time. With oil-based paint you should also be aware that some contain lead which is toxic if ingested, so you need to be careful when using certain oils on furniture that will be used by children.

STAIN

Stain, like paint, is available either water-soluble or oil-based. Oil stains tend to be more transparent, but must be left overnight to dry. You can choose a wood stain that will give a light wood the illusion of being a richer, dark wood, or a stain to match a particular colour.

Stain can be applied using either a brush or a soft cloth, but even strokes should be used. Be careful not to allow too much time between applications or a great deal of overlap on to areas that have already dried even slightly, as the end result will have dark, uneven lines and patches. If you plan to take a break, complete the section that you are working on before you stop.

In the United Kingdom, paints and stains are sold in litres and millilitres. In the United States, they are sold in ounces or in liquid volumes, although millilitres are often listed on the container. Here is a chart to help with basic conversion. Note: A United States pint has only 16 fluid ounces.

UK	USA
3.85 litres	= 1 gallon or 128fl oz
946ml	= 1 quart or 32fl oz
473ml	= 1 pint or 16fl oz
237ml	= ½ pint or 8fl oz

VARNISHES AND WAXES

After you have finished painting and decorating your piece of furniture, you will want to seal and protect it from chipping, scratching and general wear. The two general choices are either a varnish or a wax, although

you can also use a clear gesso to seal and protect.

Varnishes are available in either matt, satin or gloss finishes. This is a personal choice, matt being a soft, flat finish; satin, soft as well, but with a slight sheen; and gloss bringing a high shine to the finish. You will generally need more than one coat, and you must sand between each coat. A fine steel wool works well with varnishes.

When applying varnish, use a standard household paintbrush. Use smooth even strokes, in one direction, and avoid letting varnish drip or accumulate around mouldings and edges.

Wax is available in a standard beeswax, or in a variety of other finishes which will slightly change the pallor of your piece.

Wax should be applied to thoroughly dried paint with a soft cloth. The first coat should be rather thick and left to dry for a few hours before rubbing off. The second and successive coats can be thinner, and rubbed down after less time. When applying and rubbing down wax, always use small circular movements, applying moderate pressure.

BRUSHES

Choosing the correct brush is the key to executing your paintwork to the highest level of finish possible. Descriptions are given here of the different types of brushes available.

HOUSEHOLD BRUSHES range from approximately 2.5cm (1in) up to 10–12cm (4 or 5in). These are generally used for covering large areas quickly and smoothly. For most furniture projects, a 2.5, 4 or 5cm (1, 1½ or 2in) brush will be sufficient.

STENCIL BRUSHES are tubular with a flat end, and have a short, fat handle that can be gripped from the top for better control. They range anywhere from 1 to 5cm (¼ to 2in) across. Although you can use a standard brush stroke, stencilling brushes have long, stiff bristles that are better employed applying paint, over a stencil for instance, using a dabbing motion. (See stencilling techniques on page 17.)

STIPPLING BRUSHES are rectangular with a grip-like handle and can be used both to apply paint, and to lift paint off creating a variety of textural effects.

FILBERT BRUSHES are thick and soft with an oval tip. They are excellent for filling in decorative designs, and creating full, sweeping detail strokes. They work best when well loaded with paint.

ARTIST'S DETAIL BRUSHES come in a range of sizes and are primarily for creating finer details and lines. Most come to a point at the end for precision and accuracy, although brushes with a flat, angled end are also in the artist's detail range, and are particularly good for providing extra control when working along edges or curves.

TYPE OF BRISTLES: another decision you will have to make is the type of bristle to use. Sable brushes are natural bristle brushes and are considered the best, but are also the most expensive. If you plan to do a great deal of painting, they are well worth the investment. If you are just starting out, squirrel brushes are also a natural hair brush but are less expensive. Synthetic brushes are the least expensive.

Nylon bristle is the most common synthetic, but should not be used with oil-based paints, varnishes or cleaned in solvent such as white spirit or turpentine, as in some cases the bristles can melt. A new synthetic which is highly recommended is called 'sabelette'. This is an excellent alternative to a natural hair brush as it has the responsiveness and resilience of a sable brush without the accompanying price-tag.

CLEANING BRUSHES: brushes will last longer and respond better if they are cleaned and cared for. If you are using a water-based acrylic or emulsion, you should wash the brush in warm soapy water directly after use, as water-based paints dry quickly. When an oil-based paint or varnish is used, the brush should be soaked in white spirit or turpentine, and then rinsed in water.

Carefully clean the brush each time you change paint as any traces of the previous colour left in the bristles will leave streaks in the new colour application. To check, blot the washed brush on a piece of kitchen towel (paper towel) before using. Also check for loose or bent bristles before you begin to paint, as they will stray, keeping you from making smooth brush strokes, and can also fall out and stick to the paint finish. To remove these bristles, either clip them close to the top of the brush, or gently wiggle them back and forth until they pull out.

WHITE SPIRIT
Used for cleaning purposes, and to thin oil-based paints.

VARNISH
Seals and protects finished painting with a matt, satin or gloss finish.

WHITE UNDERCOAT
Seals bare wood and provides an opaque surface for applying basecoat.

MASKING TAPE
To block out areas that you do not want painted. Crêpe masking tape will stretch to curve around corners.

STENCILLING BRUSHES
Round, flat-ended brushes primarily for applying paint to stencils.

WOOD GLUE
For joining wood to wood.

CUTTING MAT
Excellent cutting surface when using craft knives or scalpels.

CLEAR ACETATE
Used as a base for making stencils.

OILED STENCIL PAPER
Opaque paper used for making stencils. Can get wet without disintegrating.

PENCILS AND PENS
For tracing templates onto wood and marking wood for placement of designs.

ARTIST'S BRUSHES
For applying decorative details.

SCALPEL (STENCIL/CRAFT KNIFE)
For cutting templates and stencils

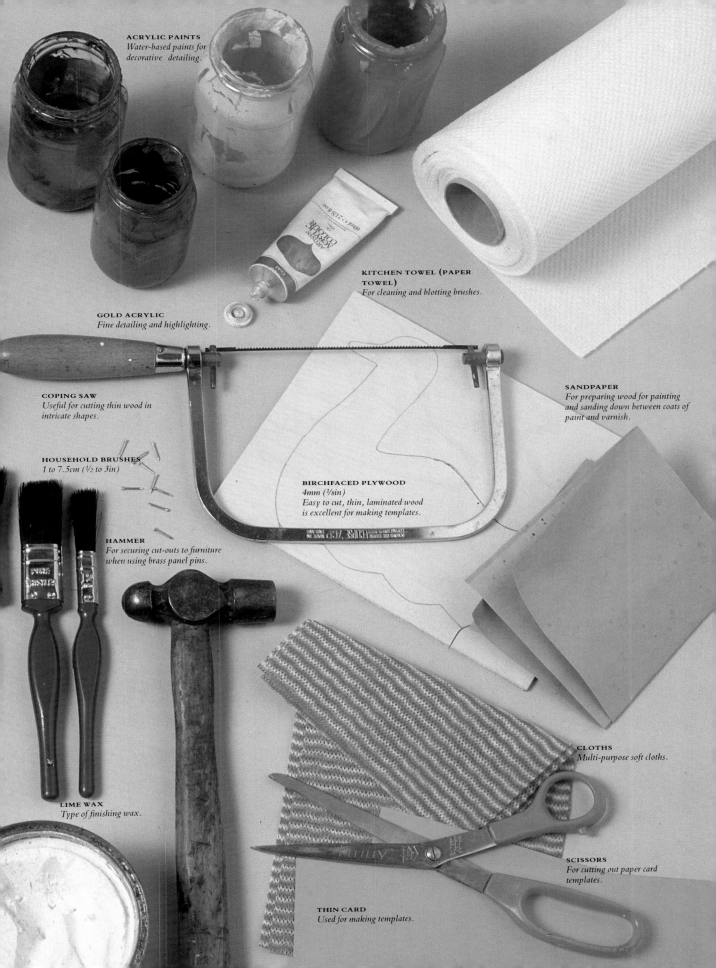

ACRYLIC PAINTS
Water-based paints for decorative detailing.

KITCHEN TOWEL (PAPER TOWEL)
For cleaning and blotting brushes.

GOLD ACRYLIC
Fine detailing and highlighting.

COPING SAW
Useful for cutting thin wood in intricate shapes.

SANDPAPER
For preparing wood for painting and sanding down between coats of paint and varnish.

HOUSEHOLD BRUSHES
1 to 7.5cm (½ to 3in)

BIRCHFACED PLYWOOD
4mm (⅛in)
Easy to cut, thin, laminated wood is excellent for making templates.

HAMMER
For securing cut-outs to furniture when using brass panel pins.

CLOTHS
Multi-purpose soft cloths.

LIME WAX
Type of finishing wax.

SCISSORS
For cutting out paper card templates.

THIN CARD
Used for making templates.

BASIC TECHNIQUES

THE INFORMATION provided in this section explains how to prepare your furniture for painting. If you are painting a newly bought piece of unfinished pine, little needs to be done. If you are decorating an older item with layers of ancient paint and varnish – perhaps even woodworm to contend with – then you will need to undertake more preparatory work. Advice is also given on choosing paint colours and a design, and how to transfer a design onto your piece of furniture. Every project gives detailed step-by-step instructions on painting a particular design, but this background information will enable you to adapt ideas and techniques from one project to another if you wish to do so.

PREPARING WOOD FOR PAINTING

When you choose your piece of furniture for painting, it will generally be either an older piece that you have found around the house or have bought in a second-hand furniture shop, or a new piece that is unfinished or 'in the white'. The latter will most likely be made of pine, and is sold specifically to be finished by the buyer. You can find unfinished furniture or pine shops listed in most telephone directories. Both old and new wood must be specially prepared for painting, using one of the following methods.

UNFINISHED WOOD

When you buy an unfinished piece of furniture that is ready to paint, check first that it has not been coated in a sealing wax to protect the wood. If it has, this must be removed before you can begin painting. This is easily done by rubbing with white spirit which will dissolve the wax, and then follow by sanding with fine sandpaper. If the piece is unwaxed, wipe down with a damp cloth or white spirit and follow with a light

sanding to remove any roughness. Do not use a wet cloth, as water will sink into the grain and could warp the piece. The piece is now ready to be undercoated as for old wood.

OLD WOOD

GOOD CONDITION: older pieces of furniture take more preparation and consideration than new ones. If the piece is in good condition, and the paint or finish is still relatively unmarred, you can give the entire piece one or two good coats of gesso. This works as a sealant, sealing the piece and creating a smooth surface to work on. Be sure that you lightly sand over the entire piece after each coat has dried with either a fine-grade sandpaper, or wire wool. Gesso can be bought in most artists' materials shops, and is available in a variety of matt and opaque paint colours. It acts as a basecoat as well as a sealer and undercoat, and can also be added to water-based paints to give them extra strength and resilience.

POOR CONDITION: if the piece is not in good condition, it will need to be completely stripped of any existing wax, paint or varnish. The best way to do this is by dissolving the old finish with a liquid stripper, which can be bought in most paint and hardware stores. Follow the directions given as each brand will be slightly different. It may take several applications of the stripping agent to get down to the bare wood. It is a good idea to use protective gloves and a mask while working with solvents.

FILLING: you will want to have the smoothest surface possible to paint on. If the piece has any gashes or deep scars, you can buy an all-purpose wood filler which

*Spread wood filler over
any gashes with a knife.*

· · · · · · · · · · ·

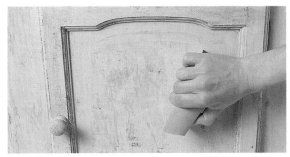

*Sand thoroughly before
painting and in between coats.*

· · · · · · · · · · ·

can be applied, and when dry, sanded smooth with the rest of the piece. Follow the instructions for the particular product that you buy.

WOODWORM: if you are using an old piece of furniture, check carefully for woodworm. This will manifest itself in the form of tiny holes in the wood. If you do not take care of this, it will eventually weaken the piece irrevocably and can also spread to other pieces of wooden furniture in the house and to wood floors. You can buy wood de-worming product at most hardware and paint stores; it will come in a can with a long, thin, tubular applicator, and needs to be injected into every hole. Do this systematically so that you don't miss any holes.

SANDING: it is important to sand before painting, and between every coat of paint or varnish that you apply. Sandpaper comes in a range of textures, but for the purposes of furniture refinishing, medium, fine and fine 'wet and dry' are sufficient. You will only need medium paper for smoothing coarse, bare wood and for use after using a filler. For sanding in between coats, and before you place a first coat on the bare wood, a fine sandpaper smooths surface imperfections, but still gives the wood, or the previous coat of paint, a mildly abrasive surface which will be more accepting to the next coat. Wet and dry paper is a bit finer than the fine variety and when used with a little water gives you an extra smooth, satin finish. Steel or wire wool can be used for smoothing mouldings, rounded legs, and other areas that are difficult to treat with stiff sandpaper. For flat surfaces, it is helpful to wrap your

sandpaper around a small block of wood. This will allow you to apply even pressure to all areas. Most importantly, when sanding, remember to sand following the direction of the grain of the wood.

UNDERCOAT: after the wood has been prepared, one or two coats of an emulsion, gesso, or mixture of the two will seal and protect the wood. White is generally used, as it provides an opaque base so that the grain does not show through the colour basecoat, and the basecoat colour itself is not affected. Staining, and some 'distressing' techniques, will not require an undercoat.

CHOOSING COLOURS

When choosing colours for furniture, it may help to consider the décor of the room in which you are thinking of placing the finished piece. What colours are in the furniture you already have? You don't have to feel limited to using the obvious colours. For instance, a fabric on a sofa may have some very bold colours in the pattern, and then some very subtle ones. Those subtle colours are still part of the décor and decoration of the room. Choose a few colours that you might like to use for background, or would just like to include in the design, and hold them next to each other. Then go through the colours that you feel will complement these base colours. If you are working with a particular décor as your basis, don't feel that you can only use colours already in the room.

If you have a particular pattern in mind, think about how your colours will work within the design. And remember, there is no law that says that leaves have to be green, or that lemons have to be yellow. Use your

imagination, experiment, and have fun. If you find that you don't like something, you can always sand it off, or cover it over with a coat of white emulsion or gesso, and start again.

The colours specified in the Project section were chosen by the artists for those particular pieces, but any or all of these colours can be substituted with others more suitable to your taste or décor. Also remember that individual paint colours are sold in un-limited numbers of shades. Be sure to check that the red, blue, and even white that you have chosen is the right shade of that colour before you get it home. There may also be slight differences between colours called by the same name, but made by different manufacturers.

MIXING COLOURS

You can mix paints to obtain different colours or shades. Red, yellow and blue are the primary colours that are mixed to create every other colour. Most paint and artists' materials shops sell 'colour wheels' which show which colours are mixed together, and in what pro-portions, to create others. Adding white can either be used to soften colours slightly, or used in a larger quantity to create pastel shades. Always add your colours together gradually. Choose one as a base, and add the other slowly, mixing as you go until you get the desired intensity. Be sure when you mix paints, that oil-based colours are only mixed with others that are oil-based, and that water-based are only mixed with water-based paints. If you find that the mixture is too thick to paint with, oil-based paints can be thinned with white spirit, and water-based with water. Again, these should be added gradually until you achieve the desired consistency.

Try to anticipate how much paint you will need if you are mixing colours. If you run out in the middle of a background coat, for instance, you may not be able to re-mix to the exact shade that you began with, and will have to repaint the entire piece. It is better to have too much than too little. Mix paints in a jar with a lid, and you can always put the extra away to use another time.

CHOOSING TREATMENTS, PATTERNS AND DESIGNS

The way in which you decide to paint your piece of furniture is generally dictated by both the style of the furniture itself and the décor of the room you plan to put your furniture in.

It is misleading to generalize by saying that smaller pieces of furniture won't accept big, bold patterns as well as larger pieces, or that on larger pieces, a small delicate design may be lost to the size of the piece. The work in the Gallery section (pages 18–27) is a perfect example of the new era in painted furniture design that says that there are no rules. What can be suggested is that if a room has a number of busy or boldly treated accents, it may be better to use a subtle design treat-ment, possibly one with very little or no detailed decoration. If the room is more solid, choose a pattern or decoration that complements the décor but makes the piece a focal point of the room as well. If you are having difficulty coming up with a decorative treat-ment that you like, think about what is around the room. Furniture and clothing fabrics, plates and silver-ware patterns are great sources of inspiration. You can also find specific books that are devoted totally to pat-terns in every style that you can imagine. If you find a design that you feel will be too complicated to copy freehand, have it photocopied. Things often look less complicated in black and white, and you can work directly off the copy in most cases, using the stencil, template and carbon transfer techniques described on page 17. You could also have a small pattern or design enlarged or a large one reduced to meet your particular needs.

TEMPLATES

Templates are guides used to trace around in order to transfer a design or image onto a piece of furniture for painting. By using them to transfer a series of images, you can create many different types of patterns. Two different techniques for making templates are described in this book; one using thin paper card, and one using birchfaced plywood.

Bold shapes, and objects which are the same on both sides when divided in half, such as flowers and leaves, make the best sources for templates. You may wish to draw your idea on paper first, then paste the drawing directly onto folded card or plywood. The drawing can then be used as a guide to cut around. It may also be helpful to measure the surface that you wish to paint, and then make a quick rough sketch of your

GALLERY

THE FOLLOWING pages showcase the work of professional artists and designers who have successfully achieved the marriage of aestheticism and functionalism that is characteristic of furniture painting. The styles and techniques are as varied as the sources for inspiration, and you will see how each artist has instilled a touch of their own personality, transforming ordinary pieces of furniture into works of art. This work is not meant to set a level of standard that should be aspired to, but will hopefully encourage you to seek out your own personal sources of inspiration and treatment.

Venetian Corner Cupboard
PORTA ROMANA
A painting by Canaletto was the source of inspiration for this corner cupboard. The cupboard was made up of old pine, and the artist applied as many as fifteen coats of varnish, sanding between each coat to give a smooth, glass-like finish to the wood.

Bogdani Box

PORTA ROMANA

Porta Romana is the product of Sarah Sturley's exceptional talent. Using either antique furniture or having pieces built to meet her needs, she creates beautiful transformations of ordinary objects. Her inspiration is varied, although her work shows a very strong classical influence, as can be seen in this chest, inspired by the painter Jacob Bogdani.

Tapestry Birds

PORTA ROMANA

The inspiration for this attractive and unusual fireplace came from a seventeenth-century tapestry from the Loire. The artist worked in oil paints and used many layers of coloured lacquer to give the piece an aged look.

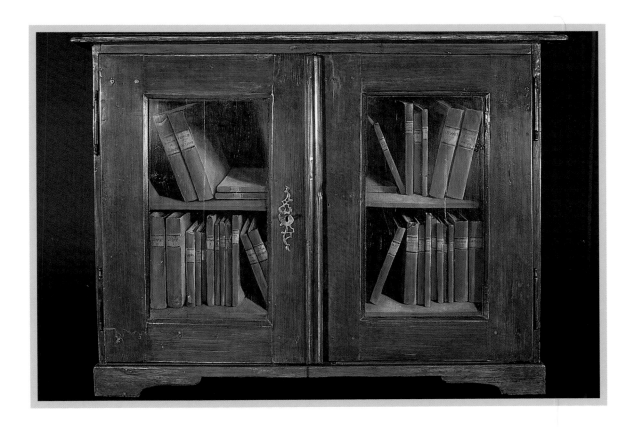

Trompe l'oeil Cupboard

PORTA ROMANA

Sarah Sturley has become well known for her trompe l'oeil work. This 'book' cupboard is a clever disguise for what is actually a television cabinet, and is created with such precision that the viewer is easily tricked on first, and even second, glance.

Tuscan Landscape Fireplace

HOYES FIDLER PARTNERSHIP

Rebecca Hoyes and Alice Sheppard Fidler find their greatest inspiration lies in classical painting and architecture. Their painting technique, using a combination of gesso and oil glaze mixed with fast-drying acrylic, is itself a classical form of treatment. This provides a richness to their work that can be seen in this fireplace.

Kitchen Chest of Drawers

GABRIELLE SABRAN

Gabrielle Sabran began painting furniture after becoming increasingly discontented with two-dimensional painting, feeling the need to find a new outlet for her work. She decided to experiment with a three-dimensional canvas, and now often makes use of the three-dimensional quality to achieve interesting effects, as can be seen in this chest of drawers. She uses existing furniture and also alters pieces to enhance her painted work.

Fruit Side Cupboard

GABRIELLE SABRAN

This cupboard illustrates the artist's love of colour and her bold, personal style. A combination of acrylics and oils gives her the unlimited colour palette she needs for her vibrant creations.

Half-Dresser

DAVE AND KAYE BALL

Dave and Kaye Ball worked on decorative interiors and stencil designs for a number of years, and became interested in the rich ancestry and techniques of decorative furniture. They are very influenced by the old Pennsylvania Dutch furniture, as can be seen in this half-dresser.

Jungle Chest of Drawers

JENNY NEWMAN

Jenny Newman first applied her painting skill and talent to furniture as a favour to friends, who wanted to convert an old dresser to something special for their child's room. Her paint brush has since touched a variety of pieces of furniture, designing each piece to take the individual interests or hobbies of her clients into account. Using the same techniques and materials employed in her painting, she converts each dresser, wardrobe or chair into an accepting canvas. This brightly painted chest of drawers shows her bold use of colour, so popular with children.

Sideboard

DAVE AND KAYE BALL

This handpainted sideboard is also influenced by the Pennsylvania Dutch style of painting. The aged look has been achieved as shown in the Dutch Folk Cradle project on page 78.

Backgammon Table Top

MOLE BROWN

Mole Brown studied decorative arts at the City and Guilds College of Art and Design in London. Since her degree, her work has ranged from decorative wall painting, to wall clocks, to backgammon table tops, as seen here. The decorative designs themselves have been heavily influenced by her travels in India and Nepal, and the colours expressive of those seen during her travels through the West Indies.

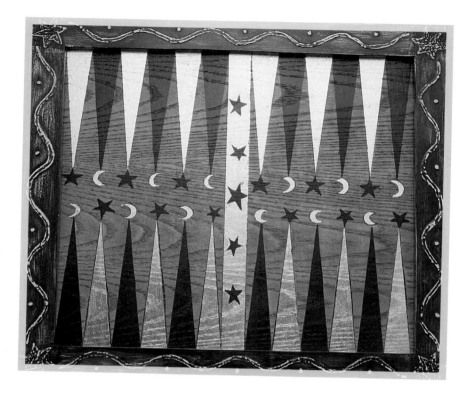

Animal Chest of Drawers

MOLE BROWN

This amusing jungle scene is depicted by the artist in a naive style, using bold, earthy colours. She has made use of the drawers to illustrate the habitat of the animals – the tree-living animals are on the top drawer, the land animals on the centre, with the water-loving fish and crocodile at the bottom of the chest.

Jester's Chair

SARAH GREAVES
STEWART

American artist Sarah Greaves Stewart creates designs that are not only unique, but seem to have a visible energy. Her interest in painting furniture developed out of a desire to find a way in which to combine interior design with fine art. Furniture offered a three-dimensional canvas which could become an integral part of the home environment.

Caridad

SARAH GREAVES
STEWART

This small stool was painted while the artist was living in Spain, and shows a vibrant, Spanish influence.

Going to Jupiter

SARAH GREAVES
STEWART

This unusual chair was the result of a dream. It was painted in acrylics, as the water-based paint dries more quickly than the oil-based, and the extensive drying time would have detracted from the excitement of the new creation.

Shaker-style Food Cupboard

SOMERSET COUNTRY FURNITURE

This large kitchen cupboard/writing bureau draws inspiration from the beautiful but simple furniture design of the Shakers. The fruit motif is handpainted, and is adapted from the old Pennsylvania Dutch style of painted furniture.

Trompe l'oeil Table Top

ROSIE FISHER

Rosie Fisher's furniture painting career began when she tried finding sturdy, practical furniture that was also attractive for her growing family. She has now developed her hobby into a thriving business called Dragons of Walton Street.

Kitchen Larder

SOMERSET COUNTRY FURNITURE

Somerset Country Furniture began as restorers of antique furniture, but in the last few years have begun to produce their own reproduction pieces, based on old country furniture from Europe and the United States. They use a variety of painting techniques to create the aged or 'distressed' appeal of genuine weathered antiques, as can be seen in this kitchen larder.

Nursery Trompe l'oeil

ROSIE FISHER

This is a fine example of trompe l'oeil. The artist has created a very believable three-dimensional illusion of children's toys and books. This would be ideal in a nursery, where the child could enjoy personalized scenes of his or her own favourite toys or personal possessions.

Children's Chest of Drawers

JILL HANCOCK

Jill Hancock's work is characterized by her bold use of colour and simple, striking shapes. This chest of drawers was handpainted, and wooden shapes were painted and attached, as shown in the techniques described in the Toy Box project on page 42.

BORDER TABLE

DAVID HANCOCK

TABLE TOPS make excellent painting surfaces. They are easy to work on, and do not restrict your design by requiring you to work around intricate mouldings and corners. This table has the added feature of interestingly shaped legs. The square section at the top of each leg is the perfect place to extend part of the border design from the top, giving the table a very pleasing overall decorative appearance.

A template was used to execute the consistent pattern repeat. This is a relatively uncomplicated yet effective method for transferring both simple and complex designs onto any piece of furniture. Templates are particularly effective when used on objects with an ample surface area. The template design can then be traced a number of times in order to create a pattern such as the one bordering this table top.

1 Prepare the table for painting according to the instructions on page 14. When the wood is cleaned and prepared, coat with one layer of white undercoat, and allow to dry thoroughly. When painting a table, it is helpful to turn the table over and paint the legs first, working on the top after the legs have dried.

2 Using the 4cm (1½in) household brush, give the entire table one coat of background colour. Choose a background that complements the colours that you are using in your border decoration. It is often best to choose either the lightest colour that you have used in your decorative pattern, or a neutral colour that is used in the pattern such as white, or grey as was used in this project. This will ensure that the decoration will remain the focal point of the piece, and by using a colour for the background that is used in the design, it will give the piece an overall continuity.

3 A template ensures consistency in your pattern. To make a template for your border decoration, take the image that you have chosen for your template and divide it in half so that you have two equal sides. Fold your piece of thin card in half as well. Draw half of your image onto the card, matching the centre line that you have drawn through your image to the folded edge of the card. Cut out the pattern with scissors. (See page 16 for hints on making and using templates.)

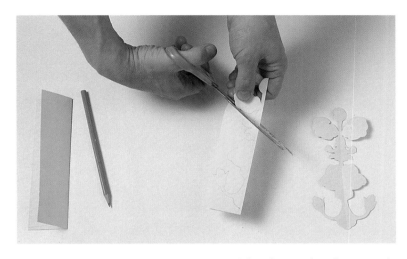

4 Using the template, lay out and trace your pattern onto the table top with a pencil. It may help to measure out the entire pattern before you begin to trace. To do this, lay the template down and make a very light mark at either end. Move the template along until you have marked all the way around the border. This will ensure that each element of your pattern is placed so that all of the elements fit into the completed border design correctly. By measuring out the design first, you can make any adjustments necessary without having to erase and possibly repaint the entire background.

Don't forget that you can use parts of the template to continue the design on the legs, and to connect the border pattern at the corners. Part of the template was used to create the designs at the tops of the table legs, and another part was traced to connect the border pattern on the table top itself.

5 The background colour for the border is painted in before the actual decorative pattern. This is done so that if any mistakes are made, the decoration will not be marred. When the background has dried thoroughly, paint over the pencilled border pattern with white acrylic using a No. 2 artist's detail brush. Your colours will appear much brighter and more vibrant over white, especially lighter colours which tend to become muted when applied over a darker or coloured base.

6 Continue to paint the white acrylic on the legs of the table. If you are finding it difficult to control the brush around the edges of the pattern, try a detail brush with an angled, flat end which will help to create smoother, more controlled lines.

7 For the painting of the border decoration itself, use bold colours, blocking in the basic shapes within the pattern. Allow each colour to dry before you use another colour next to it. This is so the colours don't blend or smudge when they meet at the edges. If you are using the same brush for more than one colour, carefully wash the brush each time you change paint, as any traces of the previous colour left in the brush will leave streaks in the new colour application. To check, blot the washed brush on a piece of kitchen towel (paper towel) before using.

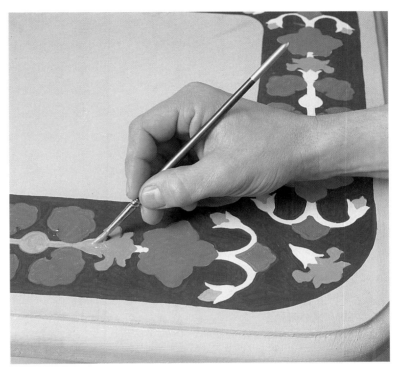

8 To add the finishing details, wait for the basic pattern to dry thoroughly, and then, using a fine detail brush that is well loaded with paint, although not dripping, make sweeping strokes allowing the motion and shape of the brush to dictate the details that you create. Try practising on a piece of paper, allowing the bristles to spread with the weight of the paint on the end of the brush. Touches of gold acrylic can be applied with a very fine detail brush to create highlights when the rest of the pattern has dried.

Finish with a matt varnish over the entire piece.

FLORAL BED

JILL HANCOCK

AN IMAGINATIVELY painted bed will easily become the centrepiece of the entire bedroom. This bed in particular, with its whimsical ducks and brightly painted flowers, is sure to become a family treasure.

Although the border and many of the details are hand-painted, the techniques for creating this design are as simple as they are effective. A template is used for the more complicated flowers; and the ducks, with their wonderful relief effect, are actually attached after they are decorated.

The sheer size of the piece may make the project seem rather daunting, but the surfaces are flat and therefore excellent to work on, and the simplicity of the painting techniques employed makes it both quick and enjoyable, even though the finished product looks as if it was difficult and time-consuming.

～

MATERIALS AND EQUIPMENT

● *standard double bed* ●
*1 litre (32fl oz) of white
undercoat* ● *500ml (16fl oz)
of grass green vinyl matt
emulsion* ● *1 litre (32fl oz) of
green vinyl matt emulsion* ●
*60ml (2fl oz) of acrylic paint
in each of the following: light
green, sky blue, navy blue,
yellow ochre, red, and gold.
These colours were also mixed
to create other colours used in
the design such as cream and
orange.* ● *5cm (2in)
household brush; range of
artist's detail brushes;
stippling brush (optional)* ●
*4mm (⅛in) birchfaced
plywood* ● *pencil* ● *coping
saw* ● *white glue or 12 brass
panel pins* ● *1 litre (32fl oz)
of poly-gloss varnish* ● *fine
sandpaper*
. . . . .

1 Prepare the bed for painting according to the instructions on page 14. When the wood is cleaned and prepared, apply two coats of white undercoat, allowing the first to dry before applying the second, and making sure that all areas are covered. After each coat has dried, sand the entire piece lightly with fine sandpaper or wire wool to create a smooth finish, taking care not to remove patches of paint.

2 Using a 5cm (2in) household brush, paint a thin coat of slightly watered down, grass green vinyl matt emulsion over the front panel of the bed. Before this dries (and as it is watered down it dries very quickly), use either the end of the brush you are already painting with, or a special stippling brush with stiff bristles, to dab the wet paint to create a grass–like effect.

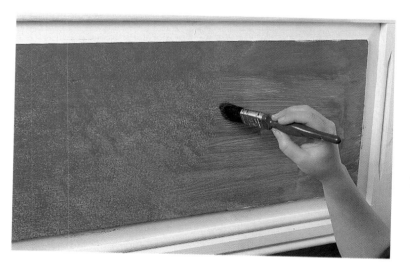

3 When the 'grass area' has dried, the tree-line can be created by applying forest green acrylic with a thick detail brush, using short but sweeping strokes. While the forest green is still damp, light green and yellow ochre acrylic can be blended in to highlight some of the leaves.

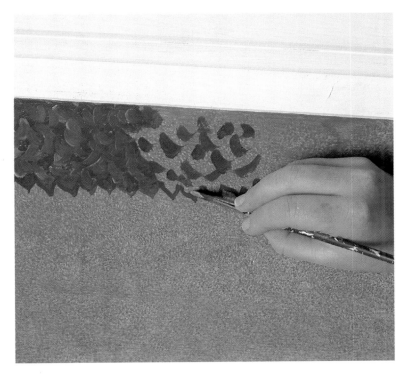

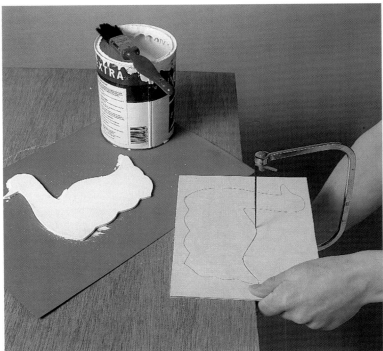

4 The iris template and the ducks are both drawn freehand onto pieces of birchfaced plywood, cut out with a coping saw, and then sanded with a medium-grade sandpaper until the edges are smooth. The iris template can be made from thin paper card instead of wood and cut with scissors or a scalpel.

If you don't feel comfortable with your freehand drawing ability, find a flower design which when folded in half is the same on both sides, and use the paper card template technique described on page 16. The ducks can also be painted directly onto the bed using the wood form as a template.

5 Measure and trace the irises onto the bed, making sure you leave enough space between them to fit the ducks in. If you make a light mark on either side of the template, at each place you plan to position a flower, before making the final traces, you can do any repositioning necessary as you have not fully marked the paint.

6 At this point, it is necessary to paint in any area that is going to receive painted decoration with one layer of white acrylic. This includes painting in the traced irises, the apples in the tree-line, and the water-line at the base. If you have decided to paint the ducks directly onto the bed, they must be blocked out themselves in white as well. If not, the wooden cut-outs need to be coated with one layer of white. Don't forget that you can see the edges of the wood when the ducks are attached to the bed, so they should be painted as well.

7 When the white paint is dry, paint in the water-line, the irises, and the apples in solid blocks of colour. While the apples are still damp, blend in a touch of the yellow ochre to highlight and give them fullness and depth.

8 To paint the daisies, first paint the yellow centres by lightly touching the tip of the brush to the surface, and then painting thin white lines out from the centres for the petals. If you want to be more exact, use a pencil to make a small mark where you want the daisies to be painted. Remember, if you are attaching the ducks at the end, you don't need to paint daisies in the spaces that the ducks will be covering over.

9 The border detail simply requires painting a strip of blue, waiting for that to dry, and then painting in a row of dark green triangles and daisies over the top. Paint in the orange borders as well.

10 The final painting touch is to outline the leaves and detail the outer borders with gold acrylic. Notice how the use of the gold detail on the bed-posts along with some of the other colours from the decorative design gives a very complete overall effect.

11 Now you can go back and decorate the ducks. Remember to allow each colour to dry thoroughly before applying another colour over it. Using slightly different colour combinations on each duck, or alternating two colour patterns will give the bed a livelier look.

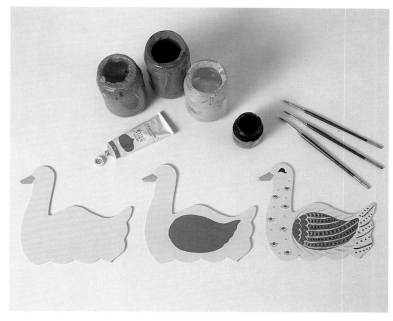

12 When the ducks have dried, attach them to the bed using either white glue or brass panel pins.

To seal and protect the paint, give the entire bed one coat of a standard poly-gloss varnish. Try to cover evenly, being careful not to let the varnish accumulate around the edges of the wooden ducks, or to leave drip marks in the finish.

9 Alternatively, if you don't wish to use the wooden cut-outs as described in the following step, you can paint the animals directly onto the box. Use a card or wood template, trace the animals onto the box and paint them with white acrylic, allowing it to dry thoroughly before you begin decorating.

10 When the cut-outs are decorated and have dried thoroughly, attach them to the box with brass panel pins. Be sure that they are secure, as children will inevitably try to get their fingers behind them and pull them off. You may wish to use white glue as well as the panel pins for extra strength. As a final detail, you might personalize the toy box with the child's name, or a label such as 'DAVID'S TOYS'.

When you are completely finished and all the paint has dried thoroughly, give the entire box one coat of a standard poly-gloss varnish to seal and protect the paint. Try to cover evenly, being careful not to let the varnish accumulate around the edges of the wooden animals, or to leave drip marks in the finish.

LEMON-PAINTED
TABLE

JANE BROSSARD &
SANDRA KRIVINE

SMALL WOODEN tables are very easy to come by, as well as inexpensive. Instead of draping them with a circular tablecloth, use paint to give an individual look. This table has been transformed from a forgotten relic into a lovely addition to any garden or sun room.

Colourful fruit stencils were used for the designs on the border and legs, and the weathered or 'distressed' look is easily achieved with a fine-grade sandpaper and a delicate hand. The legs were entwined with ribbon stencils and contrasting coloured bows were added to the crossbars as a finishing touch. You can keep to conventional colours for the fruit or choose your own colour scheme.

MATERIALS AND EQUIPMENT

● *wooden table* ● *1 litre (32fl oz) white undercoat* ● *1 litre (32fl oz) blue emulsion (gradually add white emulsion, and water if necessary, until you achieve a satisfactory pale blue colour)* ● *grey emulsion* ● *60ml (2fl oz) acrylic paint in each of the following: lemon yellow, yellow ochre, lime green, forest green, purple, crimson* ● *2.5cm (1in) household brush; stencil brush; stencilling brush* ● *glass jam jar (for mixing paint)* ● *masking tape* ● *for the stencil: clear acetate or oiled paper, a scalpel or stencil knife and a permanent ink pen* ● *2 soft cloths* ● *matt varnish and wax polish*
. . . . . .

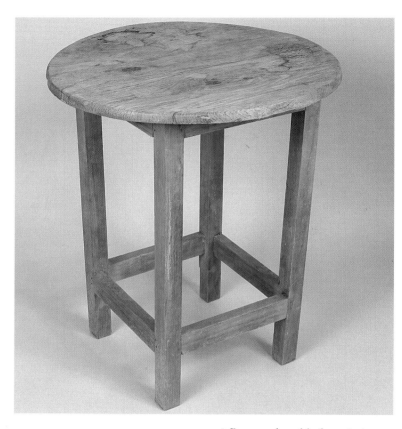

1 Prepare the table for painting according to the instructions on page 14. When the wood is cleaned and prepared, apply one coat of white undercoat and allow to dry.

When the white basecoat has dried thoroughly, sand the entire piece lightly with fine sandpaper or wire wool to create a smooth finish, but taking care not to remove patches of paint. Apply a second coat of emulsion, but using soft blue instead of white, and leave to dry.

2 The next coat of emulsion is made using mostly white, with a touch of the soft blue made earlier, and grey, mixed to your personal taste.

3 While the emulsion coat is still slightly wet, gently wipe with a cloth until you begin to see the soft blue from the second undercoat showing through. This same effect can also be achieved by waiting for the paint to dry and lightly sanding with a piece of fine sandpaper.

4 The stencils are made by tracing your chosen design onto a piece of acetate with a permanent ink pen, and then cutting the form out with a stencil knife or a scalpel. A more detailed description of this technique can be found on page 93, steps 6, 7 and 8. Before you begin to paint, use the stencil and measure your basic design onto the surface by marking each end of the stencil (in this case the lemon) lightly with a pencil. When you are ready to paint, line the stencil up with a set of your pencil marks, and tape it to the surface to keep it from moving while you paint. Use a brush to dab the paint over the stencil. (Hints on stippling technique can be found on page 17.)

5 When the lemons have dried, a yellow ochre can be used around the edges to give them more depth and dimension. Reposition the stencil if it has already been removed, and lightly stipple at the edges with the darker colour.

6 For the leaves, the same technique is used as for the lemons, beginning with a lighter colour (lime green), and shading with a darker forest green.

7 When the leaves have dried, stencil in the other small fruit and flowers.

8 To achieve an aged or 'distressed' look, you can lightly sand over the painted surface with a fine piece of sandpaper.

9 As the legs of the table are very plain, a stencil cut to look like ribbon was used down the legs. A heavier stippling technique was used at the ends of the stencil (this means using more pressure as opposed to more paint on the brush), leaving the centres light. This creates a satin effect as well as giving the impression that the ribbon is wrapped around the legs of the table.

The stencilled purple bows on the crossbars are an attractive finishing touch. When all the paint is entirely dry, coat with two coats of matt varnish. You can also follow with two coats of wax polish as well for a richer matt finish if you prefer.

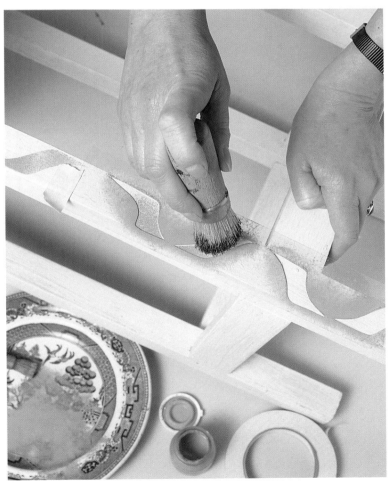

BATHROOM CABINET

DAVE AND KAYE BALL

PAINTING a simple wooden bathroom cabinet is an excellent way to brighten up a bathroom while creating extra storage space for the inevitable accumulation of creams, brushes and tubes. The colours in this piece are slightly subdued, but you can easily adapt them to suit your own colour scheme. Try looking at towels and tiles, or window and shower curtains for inspiration for your paints.

The pattern on the doors is transferred using carbon paper, and painting it is just a matter of staying within the lines. For inspiration for the patterns, try books on folk art, or special pattern books. Fabric is also a useful source. Find a design that you like and photocopy it, or combine a number of patterns to create a new one.

MATERIALS AND EQUIPMENT

● *wooden cabinet* ● *1 litre (32fl oz) of white undercoat* ● *60ml (2oz) of acrylic paint in each of the following: midnight blue, grass green, holly green, vermilion and yellow ochre* ● *2.5cm (1in) household brush, No. 4 and No. 5 sable detail brushes, No. 6 flat-ended sable brush* ● *carbon paper* ● *ballpoint pen* ● *masking tape* ● *matt varnish* ● *mellow wax* . . . . . .

1 Prepare the cabinet for painting according to the instructions on page 14. When the wood is cleaned and prepared, coat with one layer of white undercoat, and allow to dry thoroughly. When the white basecoat has dried thoroughly, sand the entire piece lightly with fine sandpaper or wire wool to create a smooth finish, but taking care not to remove patches of paint.

2 Using a No. 6 flat brush, paint the mirror frame, front borders, and door panel frames. Grass green was used here.

3 Carefully clean the No. 6 brush, and use it to paint the top architrave and the front strip of the lower shelf in holly green.

4 The design for the front panel is easily transferred by taping a piece of carbon paper to the door, taping your design over it and tracing down with a ballpoint pen. Try not to press down too hard, as you will make an impression in the wood. Also, try not to rub against the carbon while you are transferring your design, as it will leave smudge marks.

5 To fill in the design, a No. 5 sable brush works well and a No. 4 brush can be used for finer details and thin lines.

Finish with either a matt varnish or a mellow wax as you prefer. See page 11 for suggestions.

OAK-PATTERNED CHAIR

DAVE AND KAYE BALL

WITH A COAT OF PAINT and a very simple decoration, this chair is given a new identity. This is a perfect example of how the simplest treatments can render dramatic results. The unusual shape of the chair back is emphasized by the curved spray of oak leaves and acorns. You could repeat the stencil design on the crossbars, if desired.

This is a good piece for a beginner to try, especially if you choose a ready-made stencil instead of designing and making your own.

~

OAK- PATTERNED CHAIR

MATERIALS AND EQUIPMENT

● *wooden chair* ● *1 litre*
(32fl oz) of white undercoat ●
1 litre (32fl oz) of cream
eggshell emulsion ● *37ml*
(1.25fl oz) oil paint in
viridian and yellow ochre ●
2.5cm (1in) household brush;
stencil brush ● *carbon paper* ●
stencil card ● *ballpoint pen* ●
pencil ● *scalpel or craft knife*
● *masking tape* ● *matt*
varnish ● *mellow wax*
. . . . . .

1 Prepare the chair for painting according to the instructions on page 14. When the wood is cleaned and prepared, coat with one layer of white undercoat. When the undercoat has dried thoroughly, lightly sand the entire chair with fine sandpaper, dust off, and apply one even coat of base colour. Cream eggshell emulsion was used here.

2 To make the stencil, take the sketch or copy of your proposed design, and using carbon paper, transfer it to the stencil card. Acetate can be used in place of card. (For instructions to make acetate stencils see page 92 step 6.) The design is then cut out of the card using a scalpel or craft knife.

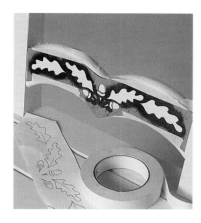

3 Position the stencil onto the chair back and secure with masking tape.

4 Place small amounts of oil paint onto a plate. Touch the tip of the stippling brush to the colour and then dab the brush tip onto a kitchen towel (paper towel) to remove excess paint before applying to the stencil. Colour should be applied in a dabbing motion rather than brushed on.

You should wait at least 24 hours before varnishing or waxing, (see page 11).

5 An alternative decorative treatment: paint with blue instead of cream, and 'distress' as described on page 81. A small leaf-motif stencil has been used.

KITCHEN
CUPBOARD

DAVE AND KAYE BALL

EVERY kitchen can use an extra storage space for the spices and jars that seem to accumulate on the counters and table. By using an unpainted cupboard, you can create a design that fits your décor as if it had always been part of the kitchen; or choose a bright pattern to add some vibrance, and make your cupboard a focal point of the room.

Look for inspiration for your design in tea towels, oven gloves, and plate patterns; and for colour suggestions, try wall tiles, plates, and curtains.

MATERIALS AND EQUIPMENT

• *kitchen cupboard* •
*stripped pine stain or stain of
your choice* • *500ml (16fl oz)
white undercoat* • *500ml
(16fl oz) lemon yellow
emulsion (mixed with white
emulsion to create the desired
lighter yellow)* • *60ml (2fl
oz) of acrylic paint in the
following: light blue, dark
green, vermilion, black, and
white* • *2 soft cloths* • *2.5cm
(1in) household brush, No. 8
filbert brush, No. 4 and No. 6
detail brushes* • *carbon paper*
• *masking tape* • *ball point
pen* • *matt varnish or mellow
wax*
. . . . . .

1 Prepare the cabinet for painting
according to the instructions on
page 14. As you will be applying a
stain, be sure to fill any holes with a
neutral wood filler; other types may
darken when the stain is applied.
When the wood is cleaned and
prepared, apply the stain evenly
using a soft cloth. To avoid dark,
uneven lines and patches in the
finish, be careful not to leave too
much time between applications or
allow a great deal of overlap onto
areas that have already been stained.
If you plan to take a break, finish
the section that you are working on
before stopping.

2 Using the 2.5cm (1in) household brush, apply white undercoat to the inner door panels.
Carefully clean the 2.5cm (1in) household brush, and, working in stages, use it to paint the rest of the cupboard with light yellow emulsion or with the colour of your choice.

3 As you paint, use a soft cloth to gently wipe over the wet areas to allow the stain to show through slightly. Be sure to work in small sections, as the larger the area you are painting, the greater the chance that the paint will dry slightly before you have a chance to wipe over it.

4 Using a No. 8 filbert brush, paint the beading around the edges of the door panel. A light blue was used here.

5 The design for the front panel is easily transferred by taping down a piece of carbon paper to the door, taping your design over it and tracing down with a ballpoint pen. Try not to press down too hard, as you will make an impression in the wood. Also, try not to rub against the carbon while you are transferring your design, as it will leave smudge marks. The decoration is painted in using Nos. 4 and 6 detail brushes and warm, simple colours. After the base colours have dried slightly, add darker touches to the edges of the berries and the centres of the leaves to create the effect of depth and dimension.

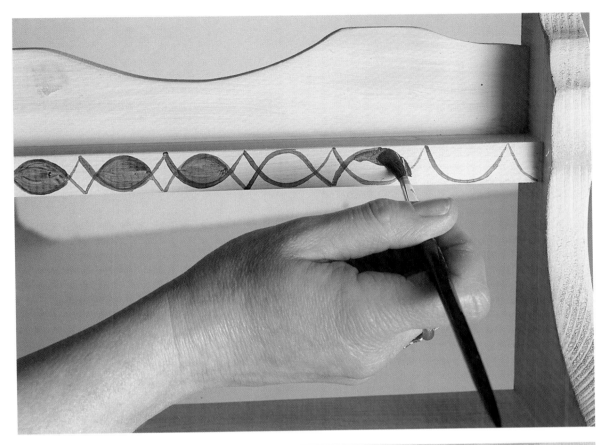

6 The top border design, consisting of overlapping arches, can either be painted free-hand or sketched in with a pencil before you begin painting.

7 Finish with either a matt varnish or a mellow wax.

COUNTRY
ARMOIRE

DAVE AND KAYE BALL

THIS full-length cupboard is treated with a beautifully subtle finish using eggshell paint and scumble glaze. The simplicity of the treatment makes it an excellent one to use on any size of cupboard.

The textured effect is easily achieved by wiping the paint with a soft cloth to reveal the basecoat. You could also apply this technique to hand-made built-in wardrobes to give them a unique hand-painted look.

MATERIALS AND EQUIPMENT

• armoire • 2 litres (64fl oz) white undercoat • 500ml (16fl oz) green eggshell paint • scumble glaze • white spirit • 5cm (2in) household brush, stippling brush, and a No. 6 flat-ended sable brush • soft cloth • white spirit • matt varnish

. . . . . .

1 Prepare the armoire for painting according to the instructions on page 14. When the wood is cleaned and prepared, coat the entire piece with two layers of white undercoat, allowing to dry thoroughly and sanding lightly with a fine sandpaper after each coat has dried.

Beginning with the sides, and using a 5cm (2in) brush, apply the following glaze mixture to the armoire: 4 tablespoons of scumble glaze, 2 tablespoons of green eggshell paint, and 4 tablespoons of white spirit. Everything except the top and bottom architrave, and the door panels, should be coated in the glaze mixture.

DUTCH FOLK CRADLE

DAVE AND KAYE BALL

A BEAUTIFUL rocking cradle or crib like this is sure to become a family heirloom. The Dutch folk motif and colours used are simple and classic, but you may wish to adapt a colour scheme or choose a design that is more fitting to the décor of your baby's room. When your baby has outgrown the cradle, use it as a store for toys or soft animals.

~

MATERIALS AND EQUIPMENT

● *cradle* ● *1 litre (32fl oz) of white undercoat* ● *1 litre (32fl oz) of vinyl matt emulsion in each of the following: tawny red, holly green and buttermilk* ● *37ml (1.25fl oz) oil paint in each of the following colours: light blue, grass green, light green, grey, white, raw umber, and yellow ochre* ● *2.5cm (1in) household brush; stencil brush; No. 4, No. 6 and No. 8 artist's detail brushes* ● *carbon paper* ● *masking tape* ● *ballpoint pen* ● *medium-grade wire wool* ● *mellow wax*

. . . . . .

1 Prepare the cradle for painting according to the instructions on page 14. Be sure to sand the entire piece very carefully as it will be used by children. You may also wish to run the sandpaper along all of the outside edges to round them slightly, making them a bit safer, and less likely to splinter.

2 When the wood is cleaned and prepared, apply one coat of white to the inside (buttermilk was used here), and one coat of a brick red (tawny) to the outside. Be aware that some paints contain lead and therefore are toxic if ingested. Check with your paint dealer when buying paints for furniture that will be used by children. A safe bet is generally to choose water-based acrylics. When the paints have dried, sand over lightly with sandpaper or wire wool, being careful not to remove patches of paint.

3 To create the distressed areas, rub beeswax into those places where there would most likely be wearing over time, such as around the handles and at the edges.

4 Leave the wax to dry, then give the outside of the cradle one coat of holly green emulsion. Allow to dry thoroughly.

5 Wearing a protective glove, use a medium grade of wire wool and rub over the entire piece, concentrating particularly on the areas where the wax was applied. This will expose patches of the red undercoat. Wipe off paint and wood dust before beginning next step.

6 Take the drawn or photocopied design you have chosen and position it onto the cradle with a piece of carbon paper underneath, and secure both in place with masking tape.

Trace over your design with a ballpoint pen, taking care not to press too hard as you may leave an impression in the wood. Before you remove the design, pull one corner away and check to see that the drawing has transferred completely. If it has not, replace the corner, and you should be able to retrace without creating double lines.

7 Begin by filling in your design with solid blocks of colour. No. 6 and No. 8 detail brushes work well for this. Allow it to dry thoroughly before you begin detailing.

8 For detailed work, a No. 4 detail brush works quite well.

9 To finish, use two coats of mellow wax which will seal the paint and give the decoration a soft lustre.

DECORATED CUPBOARD

D A V E   A N D   K A Y E   B A L L

Painting furniture generally involves the whole piece being covered with some form of painted decoration. What is often not recognized is that the distinctions in the grain of the wood can be rich decorative elements in their own right. This cupboard is a wonderful example of how a piece of furniture can be treated to bring out the natural beauty of the wood, using painted decoration purely to enhance the inherent richness of the piece.

This is the perfect piece for beginners to try, without taking the plunge of covering an entire piece of furniture with paint.

~

85

**MATERIALS
AND EQUIPMENT**

● *cupboard* ● *stripped pine
stain or stain of your choice* ●
*500ml (16fl oz) can of acrylic
paint in midnight blue for trim*
● *60ml (2fl oz) acrylic paint
in each of the following: grass
green, vermilion, burnt gold
and grey* ● *2 soft cloths (one
for stain and one for wax)* ●
*2.5cm (1in) household brush;
No. 4, No. 5 and No. 6 flat-
ended brushes* ● *carbon paper
and a ballpoint pen to transfer
your design* ● *crêpe masking
tape* ● *mellow wax*
. . . . . .

1 Prepare the cupboard for
painting according to the
instructions on page 14.

2 When the wood is cleaned and
prepared, stain the entire
cupboard both inside and out using
a soft cloth to apply the stain.
Apply the stain, using even strokes.
Be careful not to allow too much
time between applications or a great
deal of overlap onto areas that have
already been stained, as you will
end up with dark, uneven lines and
patches in the finish. If you plan to
take a break, finish the section that
you are working on before you
stop.

3 Paint the top and bottom
architraves in dark blue. A
midnight blue was used here.

4 Lay masking tape so that you leave a 2.5cm (1in) border around the entire cupboard door. Crêpe masking tape is suggested for use around curves. You may wish to measure your border first, making small pencil marks at intervals to line up your tape. Using a No. 6 flat-ended brush, paint in your border. Grey was used in this project. Do not remove the tape until the border has dried completely.

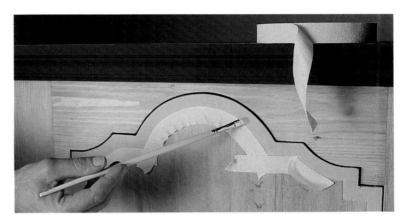

5 When the top architrave and door borders are thoroughly dry, transfer your design onto the cupboard using carbon paper (see page 17 for carbon transferring instructions). For this project, it is helpful to cut the paper that you are transferring your design from to the same shape as the cupboard door. This will help to ensure a perfect placement of the design.

6 Paint in your design using a No. 5 brush for filling in and a No. 4 brush for finer details. A wax finish over stained wood gives it a very rich, satin sheen. A mellow wax is suggested for this project, but refer to page 11 for waxing suggestions.

CORNER CUPBOARD

JANE BROSSARD & SANDRA KRIVINE

CORNER CUPBOARDS are great space savers, creating extra storage in places where the only other option might be to have a customized cabinet installed. As they are generally constructed very simply and out of wood, applying a decorative paint finish can really brighten them up. The stencilling technique illustrated in this project allows you to create a relatively intricate pattern quite easily yet looks as if it was done professionally.

Take china or furnishings as inspiration for your stencil design, or if you are less confident about designing your own then use one of the ready-made stencils that are available from art and craft shops.

MATERIALS AND EQUIPMENT

● *corner cupboard* ● *1 litre (32fl oz) of white undercoat* ● *1 litre (32fl oz) lemon, blue and turquoise vinyl matt emulsion* ● *white emulsion to mix for making paler versions of colours* ● *60ml (2fl oz) acrylic paint in peach and gold* ● *4cm (1½in) household brush; artist's detail brush* ● *glass jam jar (for mixing paint)* ● *masking tape* ● *a ready-made stencil or to make your own: clear acetate or oiled paper, a scalpel or stencil knife and a permanent ink pen* ● *stencil brush* ● *2 soft cloths* ● *matt varnish and lime wax polish or* ● *crackle varnish and 'raw umber' oil paint (optional)*
· · · · · ·

1 Prepare the corner cupboard for painting according to the instructions on page 14. When the wood is cleaned and prepared, apply one coat of white emulsion, making sure that all areas are covered.

2 When the white basecoat has dried, sand the piece lightly with fine sandpaper or wire wool to create a smooth finish, taking care not to remove patches of paint. Paint the cupboard with pale lemon emulsion. Begin your painting on the centre panel of the door and the side panels, as they will be receiving more decoration later and will have time to dry while you paint the other areas.

7 Position the stencil wherever you wish to paint the design, and stipple the cut-out areas with a stencil brush until you get the intensity of colour that you want. Don't feel that you have to paint within the acetate cut-out, as painting onto the edges will ensure that your image is reproduced clearly. It may help to tape the stencil in place to keep it from moving.

The fruit basket design on the door is reproduced by using one sheet of acetate with a number of different elements, and moving the sheet around to 'fill' the basket. The basket itself is stencilled in before the fruit and flowers. Make sure that your design is left to dry completely before the stencil is moved to another place, as the acetate will smear the wet area.

8 The grape stencil is applied to both of the side panels. This stencil is a Lyn le Grice design. (Lyn le Grice produces a number of stencils that can be bought ready-made.)

9 When the piece is completely
dry, coat the entire cupboard
with two coats of varnish, allowing
the first to dry thoroughly before
applying the second. This piece was
then treated with a lime wax polish,
which gives it its chalky patina and
generally softens all the colours.
Two coats were used, the first
applied more liberally than the
second, and both rubbed off with a
soft cloth. It is recommended that
you try a small area before waxing
the entire piece. A beeswax polish
can be used instead if the lime wax
finish does not give you the effect
that you desire.

10 Another option for the
stencilled area is to use a
crackle varnish instead of the lime
wax. This produces the effect of
ageing, and is applied after the piece
has been varnished all over. Each
manufacturer will provide
instructions with their crackle
varnish product.

Two hints: a hairdryer can be
used to speed up the drying
process, and to give the piece a bit
more aged authenticity, and a little
'raw umber' oil paint can be rubbed
over the crackled area, and then
rubbed again with a clean cloth.
This helps to define the cracks. If
you plan to try this, practise first as
it can sometimes prove a bit tricky.
When everything has dried, wax
with an ordinary beeswax polish.

SUPPLIERS

INDEX